$2.50

SPORTS STAR

Elvin Hayes

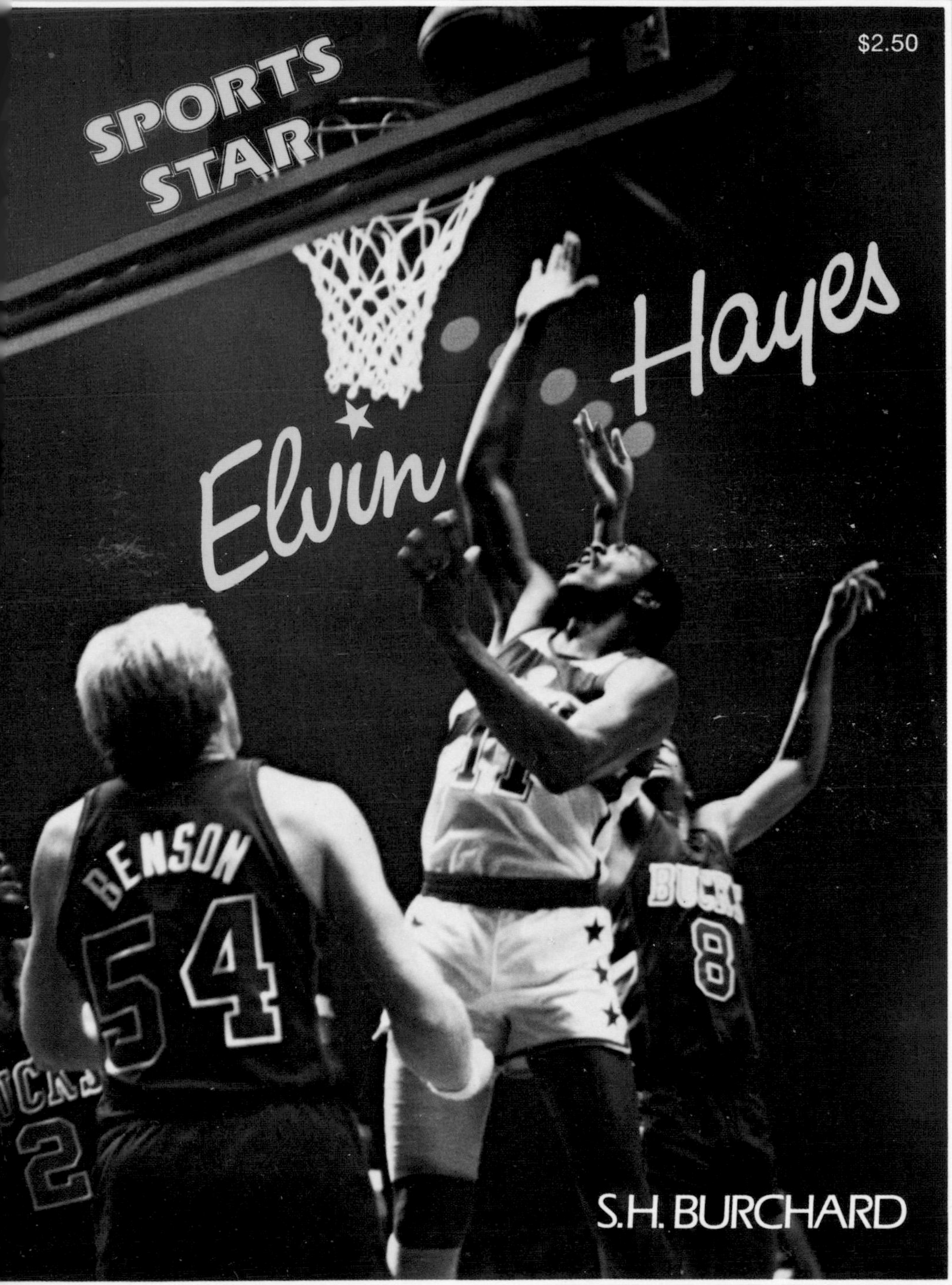

S.H. BURCHARD

INTRODUCTION

Elvin Hayes left behind a life of poverty and picking cotton when his high school basketball skills led him to the University of Houston. There he became an All-American player and ended his college career by participating in one of the most exciting college games ever played.

Being a super star, first with the Rockets and now with the Washington Bullets, has not always been easy for Elvin. As one of the greatest basketball players of all time, he has many pressures that have to be dealt with.

SPORTS STAR

Elvin Hayes

S. H. BURCHARD

Illustrated with photographs

Harcourt Brace Jovanovich
New York and London

PHOTO CREDITS
Cover: Used with permission of NBA Properties, Inc., Ron Koch
United Press International: pp. 2, 4, 36, 39,
40, 41, 42, 44, 46, 49, 51, 52, 58, 61.
Margaret Croft: pp. 6, 8–9, 10–11, 13,
15, 16–17, 18, 21, 24, 27, 28, 57.
University of Houston: pp. 30, 33, 34.

Printed in the United States of America

Library of Congress Cataloging in Publication Data

Burchard, S   H
    Elvin Hayes.
    (Sports star)
SUMMARY: A biography of Elvin Hayes from his early
life of poverty to basketball stardom.
    1. Hayes, Elvin, 1945–   —Juvenile literature.
2. Basketball players—United States—Biography—
Juvenile literature.   [1. Hayes, Elvin, 1945–
2. Basketball players.   3. Afro-Americans—Biography]
    I. Title.
GV884.H32B87   796.32'3'0924 [B] [92]   79-24286
ISBN 0-15-278018-1   ISBN 0-15-684828-7 pbk.

First edition

B C D E

CONTENTS

1 GROWING UP IN RAYVILLE, LOUISIANA

When Elvin Hayes was born on November 17, 1945, in the small town of Rayville, Louisiana, he was the sixth child in the Hayes family. The doctor said he was too weak and sickly to live, but Elvin's parents were determined to do everything they could to make sure their youngest son did not die. His father stayed up day and night taking care of the tiny baby, giving him milk whenever he cried. As a small child Elvin was not very strong, but he did live, and he and his father were always very close to each other.

The main business in Rayville was growing cotton. Mr. and Mrs. Hayes ran a cotton compress machine that pressed large cotton bales into smaller ones. Elvin's father ran the machine from seven in the morning until five in the afternoon, and then his mother took over. She ran the compress until midnight.

They felt lucky to have the job. Mr. Hayes

had gone only as far as first grade in school. Mrs. Hayes finished second grade before she had to quit and work in the cotton fields. In the 1940s life was very hard for blacks living in the South.

The cotton
compress building

When they were beginning their family, the Hayeses did not own a house. They lived in the same building that housed the compress machine. They had only a bed and a place to cook food. Their first three children were born there.

Inside the
compress building

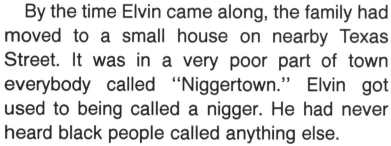

By the time Elvin came along, the family had moved to a small house on nearby Texas Street. It was in a very poor part of town everybody called "Niggertown." Elvin got used to being called a nigger. He had never heard black people called anything else.

At a very young age, like almost everybody else in town, Elvin began to work in the cotton fields. He picked cotton. He chopped it and baled it. Sometimes his white employers would try to cheat him out of his pay.

In spite of being poor and growing up in a town where blacks were treated badly, Elvin remembers mostly how much fun he had as a small boy. He had a great time playing with the pigs and chickens and the other animals the Hayeses kept at their house.

In the summer Elvin and his friends got up early in the morning to catch crickets. They

Elvin was born and spent his
early years in this house

sold them for bait, two for a penny. They
sometimes broke open watermelons and held
seed-spitting contests. When it got hot, they
raced for an old swimming hole and dived in
for a swim.

Elvin's favorite sport was baseball. He loved

it so much that sometimes, when he was supposed to be working, he would jump over the back fence and run to join his friends for a game in a nearby oatfield.

Mrs. Hayes was a strict mother. She often turned up at the baseball field with a switch hidden behind her back. Elvin had two choices. He could be whipped in front of his friends or go home and take his punishment. Sometimes he tried to run away from her.

One time Elvin thought he had gotten out of his whipping. But that night he woke up suddenly with sharp, stinging pains. His mother was giving him a licking after all.

One of Elvin's greatest disappointments was that he never got picked to play on the Little League team. He tried out every year, but the coaches said he was not quite good enough. More than anything else, Elvin

A cotton worker wearing a mask to keep harmful dust and fibers out of her lungs

wanted to own a Little League T shirt and play on the team.

At times Rayville could become a violent place. One of Elvin's first fights was when he was only seven years old. He was in an argument with a girl about his own age when

she hauled off and smashed him on the nose with a brick. Elvin ran home. He hid from his mother and tried to take care of his broken nose by himself. All summer long his nose bled, but Elvin never told his mother about it.

The children of the town learned about violence from the grownups. From morning to night, all week long, black workers worked on the big cotton farms. On Saturday night they came into town to spend their money and to have some much-needed fun. They often had

too much to drink and, to show how tough they were, got into fights. Almost every Saturday night somebody was killed. Very little was done about it.

Despite Rayville's problems, Elvin was happy there, but he also knew that someday he would want to leave. He often walked out of Niggertown and watched the out-of-state cars whiz by on Route 80. He talked to people passing through town who stopped at the gas station. He read about distant places in magazines. He knew there was a better life for someone willing to work hard to get it.

2 HIGH SCHOOL SUPER STAR

By the time Elvin was in the eighth grade, he seemed to have forgotten his dream of leaving Rayville and making something of himself. He and his friends often got into trouble. His grades got worse. Over and over he had to leave class and was sent home or to the principal's office. It seemed as if Elvin was headed for a life as a cotton worker who went to town on Saturday night and risked getting into fights or even killed.

It was a friend of the Hayes family, Reverend John Calvin, who saved Elvin from that kind of life. He was a minister and an eighth-grade teacher at the all-black Eula

Elvin's old high school has been turned into a junior high and now has several basketball standards.

Playing field in front of Eula Britton

Britton High School. He had Elvin moved into his class and made sure he behaved. Reverend Calvin also coached the eighth-grade basketball team, and soon Elvin was a member of that team.

Elvin played the position of guard. He was still small for his age. His father was only five feet five inches tall. His tallest brothers and sisters were only about five feet seven inches tall. It did not look as if Elvin would ever be very tall.

The more Elvin learned about the game, the more he liked it. That summer he gave up baseball for basketball. Blacks were not allowed to play at the fine outdoor courts at the all-white Rayville High School. Elvin would have been arrested if he had set foot on those courts.

Eula Britton High had one old wooden

backboard nailed to a light pole. The rickety rim wobbled every time a ball hit it. The playing surface was dirt.

Elvin didn't own a basketball. A few of his friends had outdoor rubber balls they all shared. He found a pair of sneakers that fit him in the trash behind the school. Both shoes were for left feet, but Elvin didn't let that bother him. All through the hot, sticky summer, Elvin and his friends played basketball. Sometimes, if they could get away from working in the cotton fields, they played for eleven hours a day. It was a wonderful time for Elvin and his friends.

Just as things began to go better for Elvin, a tragedy occurred. His father died. Since Elvin had always been closer to his father than to anyone else in his family, Elvin missed him terribly. His father had always taken special care of him and protected him. For a long time after his death, Elvin was quiet and withdrawn, but he kept on playing basketball.

As Elvin grew older, he started to shoot up in height. His mother's brothers were tall, and he began to take after her branch of the family. By the time he was a junior in high school, he was six feet two inches tall, and he grew more confident as his skill on the basketball court began to be recognized.

The indoor court at Eula Britton High was not much better than the outdoor one. The floor was made of cement tiles. There were unpadded brick walls right behind the baskets. Elvin and his teammates got used to slamming into them. They also learned to stop short in order to avoid them. The boys practiced every spare minute, and soon the team became one of the best in the state.

In Elvin's senior year, the Eula Britton team had a perfect season. They won 54 games and lost none. Stories began to spread around the South about the Eula Britton team and its super star. Scouts from all over the country

came to watch Elvin play. He could always spot them because they were the only white people in the crowded stands.

Elvin was one of the strongest high school players they had ever seen. He also had the

The gym where Elvin learned to play basketball

grace of a ballet dancer. They watched Elvin practice the shot for which he has become famous—the turn-around jumper. With his back to the basket, Elvin leaps into the air, turning in mid-jump to shoot.

The shot cannot be stopped. Elvin begins with his back to his opponent, who cannot reach the ball. By the time he is jumping and turning, it is too late to do anything without committing a foul.

In the game for the state championship played in Baton Rouge against a team from De Ridder, Louisiana, Elvin was pitted against a tough six-foot-eight-inch player weighing 230 pounds named Jessie Marshall. He was much taller and heavier than Elvin. For the first time in a long time, Elvin was scared and lost his nerve. He played poorly.

Finally the coach called a time out and

yelled at Elvin for being scared. He even slapped him in the face. Elvin went back into the game mad. He forgot about being scared and played one of the best games of his high school career.

The only problem he had was that his pants were too big. Every time he went up into the air for a shot, he could feel them slipping. He had to shoot with his right hand and hold onto his pants with his left.

Elvin scored 45 points that night, and Eula Britton won the state championship. He was voted the Most Valuable Player of the tournament.

The next day Elvin saw his name in a Baton Rouge paper. It was a big moment for him.

"Back home in Rayville," he said, "no blacks ever got their names in the paper. Never."

Elvin's high school basketball coach, Harry Lewis

Many colleges tried to get Elvin Hayes to play for them. Elvin chose the University of Houston. He liked the school and the city. The people at the school promised him they would

help him get a good education and adjust to his new life away from Rayville.

Leaving Rayville was a big step for Elvin. Though he often goes back to visit because he loves the people who live there, it can never be home for him again. Basketball was Elvin's ticket away from Rayville and from a life of poverty.

One of Elvin's high school teachers, William Moore, looks at Eula Britton's basketball trophies. Elvin helped to win many of them.

3 FAME AT THE UNIVERSITY OF HOUSTON

Five years before Elvin went to the University of Houston, one of its founders had said, "No nigger will ever set foot on this campus." Houston is a southern city and was full of prejudice when Elvin Hayes went there. Elvin and his teammate Don Chaney were the first two black basketball players in the history of the school.

Don and Elvin had never played with or against white players before they got to Houston. Both were from small towns in the South. They were used to being called "nigger" and not being allowed into some restaurants and hotels. Such treatment did not make them mad. It just made them more determined to play well. Some teams from the North, however, would not come to Houston because they did not like the way black players were treated there.

It wasn't enough for Don and Elvin to be just as good as the other players. They had to be better because they were black. Each time Elvin stepped out on the floor, he promised himself he would destroy his opponent. It is a promise Elvin still makes and tries to keep before each and every game in which he plays.

Elvin and Don worked hard to gain the respect of their teammates and the whole city of Houston. They soon became star players for the Cougars. A reporter from the *Houston Post,* John Hollis, gave Elvin the nickname he still has today. In the Navy Hollis was assigned to the giant aircraft carrier *Enterprise,* which was called "The Big E." He wrote that Elvin destroyed his enemies in the same way as the *Enterprise* did. Elvin became The Big E of college basketball, and the name stuck. Elvin was proud of his nickname.

By 1967, Elvin's third year in college, Houston was one of the best teams in the country. With The Big E leading the way, Houston fought its way into new territory for them—the semifinals

of the National Collegiate Athletic Association Championship. There they faced the awesome UCLA Bruins led by Lew Alcindor, who later became Kareem Abdul-Jabbar. Houston lost to UCLA that year, but everyone looked forward to the next season when the two mighty teams would probably meet again.

There was unbelievable pressure placed on Elvin in his last year in college. The powerful UCLA team could not be stopped. They did not lose a single game in two years. Houston, too, had to have an undefeated season in order to keep up the drama of the two super teams. Every team Houston played was gunning for them and tried to knock them out of their number-two-in-the-nation spot.

There were other pressures on Elvin besides basketball. He had to find time to do his schoolwork. Also, in his second year, he fell in love with a classmate named Erna, and they got married. One year later Elvin, Jr., was born. The pressures of basketball, school, and providing for a family were almost too much for Elvin. Some evenings he would go off by himself and lie down beside a bayou near the college looking up at the stars. He needed time to himself to relax.

At the end of the 1967–1968 season, UCLA and Houston were undefeated and ranked as the one and two teams in the nation. Elvin Hayes and Lew Alcindor were considered the two best players in the country. Both had been All-American players for the past three years.

There was enormous excitement as the time drew near for the two great teams and the two great stars to meet again. It was called the game of the century, and it turned out to be as good as everyone expected. To this day Elvin Hayes remembers it as his biggest thrill in basketball, and he can recall every minute of it.

On the night of January 20, 1968, a total of 52,693 fans were packed into Houston's Astrodome to see the game. A record television audience of some 55 million people watched the game in their homes.

There was not the usual loud fooling-around in the Houston dressing room. Each player was quietly concentrating on the big game that lay ahead. They were no longer nervous. Elvin and his teammates were confident of winning. Elvin remembers feeling very close to the other players and caring for them in a very special way. If they were to win perhaps the biggest game of their lives, they would have to do it together.

When Elvin ran out on the floor, the crowd stood screaming at the top of their lungs, "E! E! E!" At that moment, Elvin felt as if he could jump to the sky.

He almost did. The game began with a jump ball between the champion rival centers, Lew Alcindor and Elvin. Photographers crowded together on the sidelines to snap pictures of the two giants leaping and stretching to reach

the ball. Elvin won and tipped the ball to a teammate. Houston moved the ball down the floor and gave the ball to Elvin near the basket. He made the first score of the game with his famous turn-around jumper. Seconds

later Houston stole
the ball, and Elvin
scored again. This
time he made a hook
shot from the foul line.
Elvin also scored
the third basket of the
game, which made the
score 6–0. U.C.L.A.
had three players

Here Lew Alcindor
gets an edge
on Elvin Hayes
—one of the few
times it happened
in the game.

guarding Elvin, but he kept on scoring. He had 16 points in the first 10½ minutes of the game.

Houston led for the first half of the game, but U.C.L.A. fought back in the second half. The game

Lew Alcindor shoots over the outstretched hand of Elvin Hayes.

became spectacular enough to really be considered the college game of the century. Both teams played almost perfect basketball. The score was tied again and again.

With 44 seconds left to play in the game, the score was tied 69–69. Elvin was going to shoot his turn-around when he was fouled. Many fans groaned. Shooting free throws was not one of Elvin's strong points.

Elvin took the ball from the referee and looked up at the basket. The crowd did not make a sound. They were scared that Elvin would miss. But Elvin felt relaxed and confident. He made both shots. Houston led by a score of 71–69.

U.C.L.A. lost the ball on an out-of-bounds pass, and Elvin ran out the clock with the ball in his hands. Houston had won the national college championship.

Elvin scoring as Lew Alcindor
tries to block the shot.

The crowd ran onto the floor and carried Elvin off on their shoulders. He had outscored and outplayed Lew Alcindor. In one night he had become a national celebrity. Just as when he had left Rayville, life would never be quite the same for him again.

4 PLAYING FOR THE ROCKETS

Elvin won the College Player of the Year award in his senior year, and he was the first choice of nearly every pro team in the country. Not since Oscar Robertson, nine years earlier, had any college player showed such all-around ability.

Elvin wanted to play for the National Basketball Association (NBA) so he could play with and against the best players in the country. Basketball players cannot choose their own teams. The last-place teams get to have first pick of the college players. Elvin was the first

Elvin enjoys a laugh with Bob Breitbard, owner of the Rockets, after signing a contract with the San Diego team.

choice of the struggling San Diego Rockets.

That was fine with Elvin. He loved the beautiful city of San Diego. Elvin's rookie year was like a fairy tale come true. The Rockets had won only 15 games the year before and lost 67. Elvin carried them into the play-offs. The San Diego fans went wild. Stands that were nearly empty the year before were filled with fans shouting, "Stomp 'em, E!"

At the end of the season, Elvin led the league in scoring. Wilt Chamberlain was the only other rookie to do the same thing in his first year as a pro. No player has done it since.

Elvin enjoyed his new life. He became friends with Hollywood movie stars and appeared on television shows.

Unfortunately, the next three years were unhappy ones for Elvin. A few of the players were jealous of his fame and big salary. The

Elvin tries to break clear during
a play-off game against the Hawks.

Rockets began a long losing streak. Elvin was often blamed for the team's losses. Some people said it was Elvin's fault that two coaches were fired.

Elvin played the best he could, but it never seemed to be quite good enough to please the fans. Fewer people attended the Rocket games. Elvin Hayes was no longer a big attraction.

Basketball, which had always been his greatest joy, became agony for him. Because he lay awake late into the night worrying, he began taking sleeping pills. He also started having headaches and stomach aches. He even thought about committing suicide. Elvin let the management of the team know how he felt. If he was to take the blame for everything, he wanted more money.

In Elvin's fourth
year with the
Rockets, the team
moved from San Diego
to Houston. During the
summer of 1972 Elvin took
a job in Houston working for the
city's recreation program. One day,
while he was driving to an athletic
event, he turned on the radio.
He learned from a news broadcast
that Elvin Hayes had been traded
to the Washington Bullets.

5 THE WASHINGTON BULLET YEARS

Elvin Hayes was once again a happy man. The troubled years with the Rockets were now behind him. He thought the owner of the Bullets, Abe Pollin, and his wife were two of the finest people he had ever met. Elvin's greatest wish became to help the Bullets win an NBA championship for Mr. Pollin and his wife, as well as for himself.

Elvin was just as pleased with the Bullets' coach, Gene Shue. Shue let Elvin do all the scoring and rebounding he wanted to do. He told Elvin he would not be blamed if the team lost or if he missed a shot. He showed Elvin ways to become an even better player.

Elvin had been raised as a Methodist. Gene Shue was a Catholic. Elvin admired Shue very much, and some time later he, too, joined the Catholic Church.

The Bullets won the Central Division title in Elvin's first year on the team, but they lost to the Knicks in the play-offs. Gene Shue left the team at the end of the season, but this time Elvin was not blamed for the coach's leaving.

At the end of the season, Elvin and his family went back to the house they still owned in Houston. Elvin went to church every Sunday. Religion had always been an important part of his life. After a while he began to feel he wanted more than he was getting from the Catholic religion.

Elvin was uneasy about his future in general. He was a success, but in some ways he felt like a failure. He thought there must be more to life than being a basketball super star.

One Sunday Elvin went with Erna to a service at the Pentecostal Church. During the service he was called to the pulpit, and the Reverend J. L. Parker whispered a long message into Elvin's ear. He told Elvin things about his life that Elvin was sure no stranger could possibly have known. He told Elvin to go home, enter a closet, and pray secretly to God.

Elvin was very moved by the meeting with Reverend Parker. He did not go into a closet, but when he got home, he shut himself up in a tiny room. For several days he remained there reading the Bible.

When he finally came out, Elvin felt that he was filled with the spirit of Jesus and was a changed man. He was anxious to share his new feelings with others.

Elvin did more than begin to spread his views on religion. He also began to give more of his time to charity.

He never tired of visiting crippled children in hospitals, helping handicapped athletes put on their Special Olympics, and working with various religious groups. Elvin, along with a large number of other famous athletes, joined an organization called the Fellowship of Christian Athletes.

During the summer Elvin preached at various churches in the Houston area. During basketball season when he was on the road with the Bullets, he spoke from pulpits all over the country. When he retires from basketball,

This is the house Elvin bought for his mother.

Elvin hopes to become the pastor of his very own church.

Sometimes Elvin is teased by his teammates about his strong religious views. He expects and can take that kind of teasing. What he cannot take is the teasing, which

sometimes becomes more than teasing, when the Bullets lose.

With Elvin on the team, the Bullets were the division leaders from 1973 through 1977, but

Elvin surrounded by autograph seekers

the NBA championship somehow always slipped away from them. Super stars get the glory when their teams win, but they also tend to get the blame when their teams lose. No one knows this better than Elvin Hayes. His religion is a comfort, but the hurt is still there.

No one should accuse Elvin Hayes of not trying to do his best. Basketball is known for its injuries, but at the end of his tenth pro year, the 1977–1978 season, Elvin had missed playing in only five games out of a total of 892. Four times he led the NBA in minutes played. As a rookie in 1968–1969, he led the league in scoring. In the 1969–1970 and 1973–1974 seasons he led the league in number of rebounds. He is the tenth highest scorer of all time and stands seventh in rebounding. He had also played in the All-Star Game in each of his ten seasons.

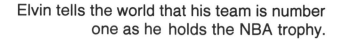

Elvin tells the world that his team is number one as he holds the NBA trophy.

Finally, at the end of the 1977–1978 season, Elvin Hayes and the Bullets achieved their goal. They became NBA champions by defeating the Seattle SuperSonics. Elvin led the team in scoring, rebounding, and blocked shots in the championship series as well as in the earlier play-offs. During the games in Washington, thousands of white cards were held up in the stands with the single letter "E" printed on them as his fans screamed, "EEEEEEE!"

The following year, during the 1978–1979 season, the Bullets were rated the strongest team in the country. True to form, they easily won the division title.

The Atlanta Hawks proved to be tough opponents in the semifinal play-off round. They nearly toppled the mighty Bullets. This time it was Elvin Hayes who was the hero of

the seventh and deciding game as the Bullets defeated the Hawks 100–94.

For the second year in a row, they met the Seattle SuperSonics in the final round, and this time they lost the championship. Elvin scored twenty points in the first half of the fifth and final game, but the SuperSonics over-powered the Bullets in the second half.

Elvin and Erna and their three children, Elvin, Jr., Erna Elisse, and Erica, returned once more to their home in Houston. It was tough to lose the championship, but Elvin had learned to accept defeat—as long as he knew he had played his best. As usual, the Big E would be back in the fall doing everything in his power to destroy his opponents and win another championship for the Bullets.

PLAYING RECORD

Team	Season	Games	Minutes	Field Goals Made	Free Throws Made	Rebounds	Assists	Personal Fouls	Points Scored	Average Points Per Game
San Diego Rockets	1968–1969	82	3,695	930	467	1,406	113	266	2,327	28.4
San Diego Rockets	1969–1970	82	3,665	914	428	1,386	162	270	2,256	27.5
San Diego Rockets	1970–1971	82	3,633	948	454	1,362	186	225	2,350	28.7
Houston Rockets	1971–1972	82	3,461	832	399	1,197	270	233	2,063	25.2
Baltimore Bullets*	1972–1973	81	3,347	713	291	1,177	127	232	1,717	21.2
Washington Capitals	1973–1974	81	3,602	689	357	1,463	163	252	1,735	21.4
Washington Bullets	1974–1975	82	3,465	739	409	1,004	206	238	1,887	23.0
Washington Bullets	1975–1976	80	2,975	649	287	878	121	293	1,585	19.8
Washington Bullets	1976–1977	82	3,364	760	422	1,029	158	312	1,942	23.7
Washington Bullets	1977–1978	81	3,246	636	326	1,075	149	313	1,598	19.7
Washington Bullets	1978–1979	82	3,105	720	349	994	143	308	1,789	21.8

*When Elvin Hayes was traded by the Rockets to the Bullets in 1972, the team was called the Baltimore Bullets; the following year the team was moved to Washington and was called the Capitals; then in 1974 it became the Washington Bullets.

SPORT STARS IN THIS SERIES

Tom Seaver
Bob Griese
Walt Frazier
Brad Park
Pelé
Franco Harris
Jim "Catfish" Hunter
Chris Evert
"Mean" Joe Greene
Nadia Comaneci
Mark "The Bird" Fidrych
Dorothy Hamill
Tony Dorsett
Reggie Jackson
John McEnroe
Elvin Hayes

PUBLISHED IN PAPER AND HARDCOVER EDITIONS

Harcourt Brace Jovanovich, Inc.

A VOYAGER/HBJ BOOK

0-15-684828-7